D0772645

Nineteenth Century America

THE
SCHOOLS

A SCHOOLMASTER

Nineteenth Century America

"THE
SCHOOLS "

written and illustrated by

LEONARD EVERETT FISHER

Holiday House · New York

[c1983]

J
370

Copyright © 1983 by Leonard Everett Fisher
All rights reserved
Printed in the United States of America
First Edition

Library of Congress Cataloging in Publication Data
Fisher, Leonard Everett.
  The schools.

  (Nineteenth century America)
  Summary: A history of schools in nineteenth century
United States, including a chapter on education in the colonial period.
  1. Education—United States—History—Juvenile
literature. [1. Education—History] I. Title. II. Series.
LA205.F52 1983   370'.973   82-18710
ISBN 0-8234-0477-3

List of Illustrations

Page

2   (*Frontispiece*) A Schoolmaster

6   Nieuw Amsterdam

9   Horn Book

11   A Whipping Post

14   The United States on January 1, 1800

17   Rural America

19   Immigrants from Europe

23   Slavery

25   Andrew Jackson

26   "Let the People Rule"

28   William Holmes McGuffey

30   Seal of Mount Holyoke College

33   Horace Mann

36   School improvements

39   Henry Barnard

40   A school water pump

43   Kindergarten

46/47   "Bleak and Desolate"

48   Plan of a one room schoolhouse

50   Geography book illustration

52   Classroom after the Civil War

57   Booker T. Washington

59   A city public school about 1900

NIEUW AMSTERDAM

I. BACKGROUND: THE COLONIAL PERIOD

Almost from the beginning of European colonization of North America through the first fifty years of American independence (about 1633–1830), formal education was designed for the privileged. Only about one of every ten children received any schooling at all.

When Nieuw Amsterdam Dutchmen opened the first free school in America in 1633, the only children who could attend were those whose parents belonged to the Dutch Reformed Church. All others were excluded. When New England Puritans founded the first Latin grammar school in Boston in 1635—a secondary school for boys about 9 to 12 years of age—only the sons from those families who could afford the tuition were admitted. There they studied Latin, some Greek, English, arithmetic, and religion with the expectation that they would become Congregational ministers. Harvard College was founded a year later, in 1636, so that graduates of the Boston Latin Grammar School could pursue their ministerial studies at a higher level. The requirements for entrance were an ability to pay the tuition and a talent for reading Latin. Later, Harvard would expand its curriculum to prepare students to be doctors and schoolteachers as well.

Until 1642, elementary education—reading, writing, and religion—was left to individual families, churches, and communities to do as they saw fit. Some did not see fit to do anything. Others sought the services of schoolmasters or simply designated one of the more educated men among them to do some teaching. In many New England towns housewives held informal gatherings in their homes to teach the very young their "letters" and catechism, a series of set questions and answers dealing with religion. These were called "Dame Schools." Usually, the only learning materials available were a Bible, a Book of Psalms and a horn book, a paddle-like board to which was attached an alphabet page, or perhaps some rhymes, or the catechism. The page was covered with a transparent leaf made from the horn of an animal, thus "horn book."

By 1642, it had become apparent that a basic education was necessary for all young people to make them familiar with the Bible, more obedient to civil and church laws, and perhaps better craftsmen, farmers, and shopkeepers. In that year, the General Court of Massachusetts passed the first compulsory education law in the western world. The law said that every child had to be taught to *read perfectly the English tongue, have knowledge in the laws and be taught some orthodox catechism.* The law did not say how this was to be done, except that if it was not done a fine would be imposed. Five years later, in 1647, the General Court decreed that towns of fifty families or more had to establish elementary schools; and that towns of one hundred or more families had to establish Latin grammar schools for college preparation. While this was not the beginning of free public education in America, it was the beginning of town and government involvement in public education. In New England, education was considered either a private matter or a church matter—and not a government matter—and many a town refused to establish a Latin grammar school, preferring to pay a fine.

The Virginia Assembly took a step in the direction of free public education. In 1646, the Assembly voted public funds to provide education for white children only. Other races of children—black and red— were excluded.

HORN BOOK

For about one hundred and fifty years, 1690–1840, the most popular elementary textbook in America, other than the Bible and the Book of Psalms, was the *New England Primer*. There were numerous editions of the primer published from time to time. All of them contained illustrated reading, spelling, and religious lessons for five generations of Americans. These subjects were taught by rote—by the repetition of memorized lessons. Usually, the constant recitation made the meaning of what was being said over and over again empty. And the verses were simple enough:

In Adam's Fall
We sinned all.

or

The Cat doth Play,
And after slay.

or

Xerxes the Great did die,
And so must you and I.

Much of this education was run by the established churches and town governments, who for all practical purposes were one and the same thing. And these church-town fathers demanded obedience while terrorizing pupils everywhere with whippings for this infraction or that mischief. Some schoolmasters erected whipping posts within the schoolhouse itself, while others planted them firmly in the ground outside the schoolhouse door.

An 1800 Boston primer reminded every student by secular and religious verse what awaited them:

> *The idle Fool*
> *Is whipt at School*

and

> *Job feels the Rod,*
> *Yet blesses God.*

A WHIPPING POST

By the middle of the eighteenth century, America's frontiers had pushed westward, the population had vastly increased, and there was more wealth in the land. No longer did the church or the British have the strong influence they once enjoyed over the outlook of most colonials. Many Americans realized that church-controlled education was altogether too narrow for life and survival in their new country, and that British control of their lives and activities was too restrictive for so big and growing a civilization.

These Americans wanted schools that taught subjects they needed to know to secure, develop, and live on a broad and often hostile continent: mathematics, surveying, navigation, science, history, and whatever else seemed useful. They believed that religious education was necessary but served only one purpose—spiritual need; and that secular education was essential for another purpose—practical need. They wanted them separated. They wanted less church supervision of general education and no British management of their lives.

A number of colonial communities wasted little time in establishing a strong point of view with respect to the direction they visualized for American education.

Academies were founded where no religious subjects were taught. The Latin grammar schools began to fade in importance. One of these academies, proposed by Benjamin Franklin, which actually grew out of a charity school founded in 1740, merged with the College of

Philadelphia in 1755. These two schools formed the nucleus of the first nondenominational institution of higher learning in America, the University of Pennsylvania.

In 1775, on the eve of American self-declared independence, there were nine major colleges or universities in the country.* Although eight of these were founded by religious groups, none of them closed their doors entirely—as they had previously done—to scholars whose religious affiliations or beliefs were different than their own. The old strict ways of Puritan Congregationalists or Church of England Anglicans no longer served the burgeoning needs of the new country. Different views were being seeded in the eighteenth century that would emerge in the nineteenth.

---

* In order of their founding: Harvard University (1636); The College of William and Mary (1693); Yale University, originally The Collegiate School (1701); The University of Pennsylvania, tracing its origin to a charity school (1740); Princeton University, originally The College of New Jersey (1746); Columbia University, originally King's College (1754); Brown University (1764); Rutgers University, originally Queen's College (1766); Dartmouth College, originally Moor's Indian Charity School (1770).

* This part of Massachusetts became the state of Maine in 1820.

THE UNITED STATES ON JANUARY 1, 1800

II. THE FIRST THIRTY YEARS: 1800–1830

The lives of most Americans hardly changed as time passed from the 18th to the 19th century. If there were any clues that indicated an old order had ended and a new one had begun, these would have been the death of George Washington in December, 1799, and the naming of Napoleon Bonaparte First Consul—dictator—of France a month earlier.

Washington was at once the symbol of American colonial defiance and nationhood, the "Father" of his country. Now he was gone as was the 18th century. Napoleon was a new figure on the world stage of politics and power. In 1803 he sold 825,000 square miles of French real estate—the Louisiana Territory—to the United States. In effect, Napoleon gave up some of the richest land in the world and doubled America's size in order to finance his European wars. And those military adventures would spin a web that by 1812 would draw the United States once again into a war with Great Britain.

On the educational scene, the founding of Union College in Schenectady, New York, in 1795, was of some interest. Union was the first architecturally planned college campus in the new United States. And there, at Union, a name pointedly signifying the joining of sovereign states into one nation, American collegiate

15

Greek letter social fraternities were originated with the chartering of Kappa Alpha in 1825. Greek letter societies were not altogether new in American academic life, however. Phi Beta Kappa was founded at the College of William and Mary in Virginia in 1776 as a secret society. Never a social fraternity, it became a scholastic honor society in the 1830s.

In any event, there were a little more than five million people living in the sixteen states* that comprised the United States on Janaury 1, 1800. That was fewer than the population of present-day New York City which in 1800 was a recognized metropolis of sixty-thousand citizens.

Nearly half of America's five million were sprinkled over the farms, plantations, villages, and towns of the South. The remainder was about equally divided between the Middle Atlantic States and New England. At the turn-of-the-century, the vast majority of Americans lived outside of the towns and cities. They were rural people, for the most part, rather than urban people, and they would remain rural for much of the nineteenth century. And for much of the nineteenth century, especially the first thirty years, lower or primary education in America would have a rural flavor.

Yet, winds of change had begun to whip across the

---

* Connecticut, Delaware, Georgia, Kentucky, Maryland, Masssachusetts, New Hampshire, New Jersey, New York, North Carolina, Pennsylvania, Rhode Island, South Carolina, Tennessee, Vermont, Virginia.

land during those first thirty years that promised, for
better or worse, a different style of life, a different set of
values, and a national growth without parallel in the
history of the world. The change was wrought by the
Industrial Revolution. Within one hundred years,
1800–1900, the industrialization of the United States
would become irreversible, and the face of the nation—
a nation destined to be a world power—would be that
of a mechanic as well as that of a farmer.

The industrialization of America would be a century-

RURAL AMERICA

long process. Nevertheless, during the first third of the nineteenth century, that process, then in its infancy, began to generate employment opportunities in factories that bore little resemblance to farm chores. Farmers left the uncertainty of their land and headed for the cities, dreaming of a better life. Immigrants from Europe left their ships at city ports and stayed in the cities, for the most part, flocking to the same factories that beckoned the American farm family.

City growth was inevitable. With that growth came an increase in crime, disease, hunger, slums, and a style of wretched living that fed on the ignorance seeded in the filth and congestion of the growing city. The movement of people toward the cities began to create more of an urban America than had previously been noticed. And while the United States was not suddenly less rural than it had been; nevertheless, it was turning from an agricultural society into an industrial one.

By 1830, there were nearly thirteen million people in what had become twenty-four American states. Three and a half million of these were scattered throughout the agricultural South. But approximately two and a half times that number were concentrated in the industrializing North—seven million in the Middle Atlantic States; two million in New England.

As the population grew and shifted, and as the country prepared itself to become a technological giant, the education of the young became an increasingly important public issue.

Education in the United States between 1800–1830 was, by and large, a private matter. Most families unable to pay tuition at church-supported or secular private schools, and who lived nowhere near a free charity school operated for the poor through private funds, were unable to send their children to any school. And there were those who believed that the fast growing class of city working people—most of whom could not afford a formal education to improve their lot in society—needed more than charity schools. State-supported education was the answer, they reasoned.

IMMIGRANTS FROM EUROPE

Without an educated citizenry, they insisted, a citizenry which considered itself constitutionally free, the country would be divided into two major classes: an upper class consisting of a very few who controlled all of the factories hence all of the wealth, and a lower class consisting of most of the people, who controlled nothing and had no wealth. The destiny of most Americans—their jobs, their homes, their health, their lives, and general welfare—would be in the hands of all too few Americans. The result would be a virtual economic slavery that would undermine the course of political freedom envisioned by the Founding Fathers and in the end destroy the very meaning of a free America.

Moreover, if the vast majority of the people remained uneducated, crime, poverty, disease, and all those distortions of life bred by ignorance would overtake the nation. Education of the general public was also necessary if the machinery of industry was to be kept running. Without education it would be difficult to acquire the skills needed to produce the goods that an increasingly industrialized world demanded. The United States could not afford to stand still or become backward in a western world moving into an industrial age.

Those who argued all these points in favor of free public education—an idea that had never been tried in the western world—supported the principle that such education could be made possible by taxing every citizen. They pressed their point of view on politicians in the hope that they would see the light and enact legislation to provide publicly funded free education.

Considering the stake that a politically free and independent working class people had in a future tied to certain dependency on a factory system, it is not surprising that those who supported free public education also supported organizing labor—unionism—for their mutual protection and welfare.

The business and monied class who held most public offices, owned the factories, and ran the country were not too excited by the prospect of public education. For one thing, the cost of the scheme would have to be borne by them through the increased taxation. Also, they were convinced that most people would gain nothing from education, whether free or not. Worse still, they viewed the working individual as being a member of a fixed low class, who, once educated at public expense, could rise from that class and threaten the order of society.

Besides, they argued, too much education of the working class would eventually deprive the upper class factory owners of workers for their factories. Once that happened, they reasoned, the country would stand still and decline, while the British moved ahead without any free public education. It was the same argument—turned around—given by those who said that the United States would surely amount to nothing if the working class people were *not* educated.

The wealthy segment of the nation supported a theory of governing that emerged during the 1700s in France, as the factory system was seen to be the ultimate replacement of farming as the bulwark of a country's economy. The theory was called "laissez-faire." It was the beginning of the "free enterprise system." The theory maintained that a person was more productive when left to his own initiative, and that government should not interfere with that initiative and productivity by passing laws to either help or hinder the worker. Left alone, the worker, therefore, would add to the economic strength of the nation. In essence, "laissez-faire" held that governments should have no say in the economic affairs of nations—that business and the making of profit or the sustaining of loss was a private matter.

The business community which popularized "laissez-faire" seemed to agree, however, that taxation was a good method for raising money necessary to keep the machinery of government running. Yet, those who believed in "laissez-faire" and who would have to bear the brunt of taxation insisted that no government should tax anyone without that person agreeing to it first! In other words, no one with taxable property should be taxed to pay for the education of those without property (and who, therefore, could not be taxed) unless he agreed to permit himself to be taxed!

During the 1820s, slavery had become a national issue. Also, trade unionism, already a national issue, had begun to demand free public education. In labor's view, education was the key to self improvement, and certainly to a better life than the American workingman knew. The southern black slave knew that too but was helpless to either voice an opinion on the matter or pursue it in any way. Freedom from slavery had to come first, and that was more than a generation into the future.

Nevertheless, the pressure of public opinion was being brought to bear on the conservative elements who would deny education to the striving multitude of ordinary Americans. And this pressure was enough to create a momentum for tax supported, free public education, and for education beyond the meager elementary

SLAVERY

level of reading, writing, arithmetic and religion. Elementary education, however privately funded, was slowly becoming inadequate as the sole training structure for the majority of Americans fortunate to have had such education in the face of the coming industrial challenge.

Moreover, the atmosphere for expanding the educational prospects of most Americans was being further enhanced by changing political styles. No longer did it seem practical or even wise for politicians to secure their offices through the patronage of a selected few. Now the politicians had to begin looking to ordinary people for support in order to realize their political ambitions.

The changing American society, joined to its agricultural past and tied to an industrial future, not to mention the tug of democratic idealism, was reaching for popular education that seemed to be reflected in the coming of Andrew Jackson, the seventh President of the United States.

Jackson was the governor of the Florida Territory when in 1821, the City of Boston, Massachusetts, established America's first public high school, the English Classical School. The English School, as it was called three years later, was not much different than the traditional academies. The education offered was only meant for a small portion of those Boston boys who needed further training for leadership roles in the growing society, and who for one reason or another could not or would not enroll in an academy. Like the academies, the English School charged tuition. But unlike the academies, the school was supported by public money rather than by private money. Although the school was hardly free, it did seem to indicate America's willingness to take a more public approach to education to meet the requirements of a changing time.

Jackson was not yet an official candidate for the presidency, when in 1827 the Commonwealth of Massachusetts enacted a law which required towns of 500 families to establish high schools, one for boys, another for girls. Soon, other towns throughout New England established similar schools.

Jackson's arrival on the national political scene in 1828 gave some impetus to the efforts of those aiming

ANDREW JACKSON

"LET THE PEOPLE RULE"

for increased educational opportunities.

Until the presidential campaign and election of 1828, nominations for the presidency originated in the Congress. In 1828 the various state legislatures offered their own candidates while keeping wary eyes and ears on the huge political mass meetings that were occurring in the cities. When Jackson was finally elected on a platform of reform and a promise to loosen the grip on government held by wealthy men, the *Age of Jackson* and the era of the *Rise of the Common Man* had begun (1829–1850).

"Let the People Rule," was Jackson's slogan. And in Baltimore, Maryland, in May, 1832, they did. There, for a second time, Jackson became his party's choice—the Democrat-Republicans—for the presidency. But this time he was not nominated by the wheelings and dealings of incumbent politicians. He was chosen by delegates from everywhere in the country. The occasion was the first national political convention convened by a political party to nominate candidates for the two highest offices in the land, President and Vice President. Jackson and his former Secretary of State, Martin Van Buren were chosen. They beat their opponents, Henry Clay and John Sergeant that November and took office the following March, 1833. Eventually, Van Buren would succeed Jackson as President.

WILLIAM HOLMES McGUFFEY

III. THE GROWING YEARS: 1830–1860

During the thirty year period prior to the outbreak of the Civil War, 1830–1860, there emerged a quality of leadership in American education that would set the tone and pattern of public education in the United States into the twentieth century.

Between 1836–1857, Ohioan William Holmes McGuffey, minister, professor, philosopher, and college president, along with his brother Alexander, wrote a series of six illustrated reading books for elementary school children. Called the *Eclectic Reader,* or simply "McGuffey's Reader," these books differing from one another by levels of difficulty sold some 120,000,000 copies. Nearly every American school child learned to read from these books until the close of the century and for some years after. Here, in "McGuffey's Reader," boys and girls were introduced to all the moral virtues that built character and made for good citizenship: honesty, charity, temperance, patriotism, cleanliness, and kindness. Pictures, words, sentences, and "pieces" taught pronunciation and usage. But the tone of morality suggested in all parts of McGuffey's Readers shaped the minds of young Americans for the rest of their lives. The final two sentences from Lesson I. of *McGuffey's First Reader* indicated what had to be done besides learning to read:

They must keep the book clean.
They must see how fast they can learn.

No other textbook in America had so durable an effect and so affectionate a hold over so many Americans as McGuffey's Readers. One could learn to read and at the same time rely with certainty upon the unswerving rules of life set down by William Holmes McGuffey.

While McGuffey was busy in Ohio, Massachusetts legislator James G. Carter was hard at work pointing out the seemingly hopeless inefficiency of Massachusetts schools. His concerns revolved around the inability of the poor to receive the most basic education necessary to prepare any American for life in an industrial world;

SEAL OF MOUNT HOLYOKE COLLEGE

around poorly qualified teachers; and around poorly kept schoolhouses. Convinced that Massachusetts schools needed supervision, Carter received enough political support to enact legislation to remedy the situation. In so doing, he created a solid footing for the development of the free public school.

In 1837, Carter steered a bill through the Massachusetts General Court establishing a State Board of Education, the first such board in the United States. He then went on to create a state fund to help Massachusetts towns improve their schools and the quality of education with supervision from the newly established Board of Education. Shortly before his death in 1840, Carter helped to organize America's first school to train people to become qualified schoolteachers. It was called a "normal school."

Elsewhere in Massachusetts in 1837, Mary Lyon opened her Mount Holyoke Seminary at South Hadley. Hardly a seminary, Mount Holyoke—to be known as Mount Holyoke College some years later—became the first independent institution of higher learning established solely for women. Although Oberlin College in Oberlin, Ohio—America's first coeducational institution—was awarding degrees to women as Mount Holyoke College was preparing to welcome its first students, the founding of Mount Holyoke as a women's institution during the second quarter of the nineteenth century reflected both the progressive response to education in Massachusetts generally, and the strong willed response of American women to male oriented education everywhere. Before the century would end Mount Holyoke would be firmly established as a leader in American education with programs in the areas of art, science, and education.

The challenge of Mount Holyoke and sister institutions that followed, including the sprinkling of girl's high schools already flourishing, was clear: that American women would not be denied an intellectual and political role in the shaping of the country. And although America's educated women marched for their rights and recognition all through the nineteenth century, it was not until the twentieth century—1920—that they entered the political mainstream with the passage of the Nineteenth Amendment to the Constitution, which finally gave women the right to vote.

While it was one matter to enact proper legislation in any field, let alone education, it was another matter to implement and enforce the new laws. Such was the case in Massachusetts with the new State Board of Education. The board was weak. It lacked leadership and direction.

Horace Mann knew this when he gave up his highly successful law practice to become head of the Massachusetts State Board of Education shortly after its creation in 1837. Over the next twelve years, Mann stirred up the state with his constant speeches, reports, and articles

HORACE MANN

concerning the miserable condition of Massachusetts *common* or public education.

Mann insisted that it was the right of every American to receive an education. But more importantly, he insisted that it was America's right to educate every child even if parents objected.

"Far better to pay taxes (for schools) ... than to build jails, penitentiaries and almhouses," he cried.

"Education is our only political safeguard," Mann said over and over again.

There were many who turned a deaf ear to Mann. Still, he kept promoting his cause in and out of Massachusetts in a storm of controversy, pushing and campaigning for the common school—for free public education supported by public taxation.

Although most ordinary people were indifferent to the academies and private schools, regarding them all as upper crust enclaves teaching useless subjects, they were just as indifferent to common schooling. They preferred their children to work on the farms or learn a trade and remain in the same level of society as their mothers and fathers, and their grandmothers and grandfathers. Education seemed to have no rewards for them.

But Horace Mann persisted. *"I say it is education ... education will give strength, competency and order ... take away education and all things will rush to ruin as quickly as the solar system would return to chaos if gravity and cohesion were destroyed."*

In addition to his basic educational theories regarding common schooling, Horace Mann stubbornly refused to recognize religious training or any religious reference, regardless of the denomination, inside the public schoolhouse. He viewed this as a flagrant violation of the United States Constitution.

Those who opposed Mann on the public school issue, principally because they did not want to be taxed for the support of such institutions, now had a handle. They criticized his idea of a public school as being "Godless." There were many who rallied around that cause. But Mann had his supporters who rallied around him for their own reasons. Among these were Protestants who feared that the rising immigration of Roman Catholics—chiefly Irish—would infect the curricula with "popish" ideas and weaken the traditional Protestant control of American society. They wanted no religion at all in the schools. Nonsectarian public education supported by public money that came from all races, religions, sects, and creeds was in the best interest of a free America. And after all, was that not what the American democracy as seen through the Bill of Rights was all about? Horace Mann could not have agreed with them more. The issue was not whether or not schools would be Godless, but whether or not schools supported by taxes from people of differing religious beliefs should be used to promote the religious convictions of one faith—even if only by a simple prayer. The battle would go on for the next one hundred and forty years with no end in sight.

Mann's term of office as Secretary of the Massachusetts State Board of Education ended in 1848 when he ran on an anti-slavery ticket for Congress and was elected. But however much controversy Mann continuously aroused, he did manage to heighten awareness and support for public nonsectarian education. He did spark movements for better trained, better qualified, and better paid teachers. He did cause public pressure that resulted in the improvement of school buildings and equipment. In the end, Horace Mann made the whole country aware of the importance of public education and tied our destiny and security to that very idea.

SCHOOL IMPROVEMENTS

In 1852, Mann ran for governor of Massachusetts but lost. He was appointed the first president of Antioch College in Ohio, and died there in 1859. A number of Mann's ideas were adopted during his lifetime, but the one that finally spread throughout the entire nation and became a law in every state was passed in the same year he made his run for governor. In 1852 the Commonwealth of Massachusetts became the first state in the union to enact a compulsory education law. It was Horace Mann who had originally implanted the principle that society had a right to educate every child, despite parental objection, for the benefit of society as a whole.

In Connecticut, another educator and contemporary of Horace Mann, Henry Barnard, was determined to improve the educational climate in his state. Like Horace Mann, Barnard was a lawyer and member of the Connecticut General Assembly. And like Mann, Barnard pointed a critical finger at the poor quality of Connecticut common schools. Barnard's crusade was based on reports of the Society for the Improvement of Common Schools, which was organized in 1827.

The society discovered that instruction was haphazard, or even nonexistent in some cases. Much of this was due to a high rate of truancy, a mixture of poor and unusable textbooks, and little else in the way of other supplies. Added to this were poorly prepared or unqualified teachers who worked for below normal wages—$14 to $15 per month if they were men, $5 to $6 per month if they were women. Worse still, the reports blamed parental indifference for all the problems. It was evident that the poor could not see the usefulness of education when the children were needed at home to work full time to keep from starving, that the middle class parents were so concerned about their own need to improve their lot that they paid little attention to the needs of their children, and that the rich who could afford private education did not have to participate in the upkeep of public education.

Nevertheless, in 1838, one year after Mann had assumed leadership of the newly chartered Massachusetts State Board of Education, Henry Barnard successfully led the fight to begin to prevent further deterioration of Connecticut's common schools. The General Assembly created a Board of Commissioners of Common Schools to implement and improve the administration of Connecticut schools. Between 1838–1842, the board inspected hundreds of schools, recommended new programs of study and textbooks, organized normal schools for the preparation of qualified teachers, organized libraries—the backbone of all quality education in a free society—and saw to it that regular meetings were held between teachers and parents.

But for all the good intentions of the board and its secretary, Henry Barnard, the road to improvement was rocky indeed. During this period about one hundred of

HENRY BARNARD

the several hundred one room school houses scattered throughout the state were inspected. These buildings measured, for the most part, about twenty feet square with very low ceilings, some seven or eight feet high. The buildings were heated either by wood burning stoves or by fireplaces. None of them had any indoor plumbing. And only three of these schools were found to have any plumbing at all—outdoors—a well, perhaps with a pump, and an outhouse. Seven of these schools were certified to be in excellent condition. About thirty of them were listed as fair and usable. The rest, over sixty buildings, were said to be in dreadful condition and unusable.

"... *decidedly unhealthy* ...", wrote Henry Barnard in his report about schoolhouses. "... *not one in a hundred*

A SCHOOL WATER PUMP

has any other provision for a constant supply of that in-dispensable element of health and life, pure air ... that the seats and desks are calculated to induce physical deformity and ill health ..."

Writing on the subject of buildings and equipment at another time, Barnard deplored the fact that desks and the very walls of the schoolhouse were defaced by students *"... marked with ... images ... which would make heathens blush ..."*

The most crucial problem of all, however, dealt with educational financing. Connecticut parents were still being charged tuition. Some expenses were paid by the state. The people of Connecticut like everywhere else in America refused to allow the government to tax them for the education of someone else's daughter or son. Moreover, and as was customary, people who sent their children to expensive private schools or academies, or no school at all—there was no compulsory education act in Connecticut as yet—did not have to support common schools.

The "rate bill" law was very clear on the matter, and Connecticut was not alone in the enactment and enforcement of a rate bill:

Whenever the expenses of keeping a common school ... shall exceed the amount of monies appropriated by law to defray the expenses of such schools, the committee in such district ... may assess the same upon parents, guardians and masters of such children.

In other words, a parent could not be assessed or taxed for the support of his district's school if he or she had no children in attendance at that school. By the same token, a childless couple, although this was not stated but merely implied, could not be assessed or taxed for the education of children they did not have.

Still Henry Barnard persisted. He pursued the idea that a property tax on all was the basis of a free school system. And a free school system was, in his view, the essence and savior of American democracy. But Barnard's program of reform came to an abrupt, if temporary, halt. In 1842, the Connecticut governor, William W. Ellsworth, a Whig, lost the election to a democrat, Chauncey Cleveland. Cleveland did not think much of Barnard's "innovations." He dissolved the Board of Commissioners and Henry Barnard's position on that board with it. Barnard, disillusioned by this turn of events, left Connecticut for Rhode Island. There he was able to effect common school reform, organize school libraries, and redesign the methods of school examinations.

By 1849, Barnard's program for reform in Connecticut had been reestablished, and he returned home to become superintendent of schools, among other education offices. In 1858 he went to Wisconsin as chancellor of the University of Wisconsin. The University was only ten years old, having been chartered in 1848, the same year Wisconsin was admitted into the Union as the 30th state. Three years before his arrival, in 1855, Margaretha Schurz had founded the nation's first kindergarten. Margaretha Schurz, a German immigrant, was the wife of Carl Schurz, himself an immigrant, who would one day become a United States Senator, a brigadier general in the Union Army, Secretary of the Interior under President Rutherford B. Hayes, and an editor of *Harper's Weekly,* a magazine.

While in Wisconsin, Barnard, true to form, interested himself in Wisconsin's common schools and contributed much to their development. He returned East in 1866 to become president of St. John's College in Annapolis, Maryland. A year later he gave up the post to become the first United States Commissioner of Education.

KINDERGARTEN

By 1860, on the eve of civil war, nearly all of America's 32 states encompassing a population of 32,500,000 people, mostly middle class or poor, had effected some central control over public education. Management of district schools was slowly but surely passing from the district committeeman—the lone volunteer miner, farmer, blacksmith or similar person—to state authorities. The states were attempting to improve the curricula, the quality of teaching, and school building maintenance by establishing teacher training schools—the normal schools—and by allocating money for instructional materials and repairs.

More importantly, the pre-Civil War public was beginning to understand the need for the abolition of the unfair rate bills and the creation of a fair, universal education tax with which to support excellent, free nonsectarian public schools. Compulsory education seemed to be senseless if those compelled to send their children to school had to pay tuition which many did not have. And since the ultimate benefit of education would be the improvement of society everywhere, it did not seem fair that those who would someday enjoy those benefits but who did not send children to public schools should be excused from supporting those public schools. Compulsory free education was essential in the minds of many if America was to assume a leadership role in an increasingly industrialized world. Moreover, the certainty and continuity of American democracy as envisioned by the framers of the Constitution was linked to the education of all, rich and poor and middle class alike. And although the rate bill system was still considered eternally fixed in the governance of schools in some northern states, most states everywhere else were seriously investigating methods of supporting free nonsectarian educational systems by public taxation.

While liberal factions pushed for educational reform, conservative elements resisted. Education was not a burning issue as the North and South debated slavery and states' rights, and prepared for war. Despite the various boards and commissions established to define and upgrade American educational goals and practices, schools remained much as they had been for years.

The clapboards and shingles of many a rural "little red schoolhouse" were as shabby looking as ever, badly in need of a coat of paint they probably never had to begin with. Every grimy window had at least one broken pane stuffed with a rag or someone's old hat. There was no front school yard, only the unpaved main road, dusty or muddy, iced solid or flooded, depending upon the season. Usually the schoolhouse was set down on an unprotected, worthless plot of land exposed to wind, rain, cold, sleet, and heat. One Connecticut resident recalling his early nineteenth-century schooling in Ridgefield described the building and area as being *"bleak and desolate."*

Large towns were divided into districts. Each district

"BLEAK AND DESOLATE"

was responsible for providing its own school for most of the pre-Civil War period. Once the school was decided upon, built, and put to use, the unpaid committeeman looked after things—property, structure, furnishings, educational materials, and equipment. It made no difference that the committeeman may never have had an education himself.

During the early years of the century, a state such as Massachusetts might have contributed $10 a year toward the upkeep of a district school. If the district politicians felt generous, they might have added another

$10. Tuition, however modest, underwrote whatever else had to be done that state and district funds left undone. And that was a great deal! Schoolhouses received hard use and were in a continuous state of disrepair. Often there were no maps, books, papers, or writing materials. Teachers were sought who would work for small wages. Usually the least qualified came the cheapest. These were, in part, the conditions that irritated Horace Mann, Henry Barnard, and others, and fired their resolve to reform American education.

The inside of a typical schoolhouse was a disgrace. The plaster walls were often cracked and always sooty from the woodburning stove that sat in the middle of the school's only room. A sloping counter for writing

PLAN OF A ONE ROOM SCHOOLHOUSE

and reading ran around the rear and two side walls. Rough long benches ran parallel to the counters. The teacher sat or stood at a high desk mounted on a platform overlooking the whole scene. The front hall of the one room schoolhouse was lined with wood pegs for the students to hang their winter outer clothing. Sometimes a whipping post was bolted to the floor of the front hall.

Textbooks were either bound in leather or wood boards, and always seemed to be well thumbed and worn at the edges. In addition to "McGuffey's Readers," America's young students learned their spelling from Noah Webster's *The Elementary Spelling Book,* originally called *The American Speller* when first published in 1783. At the time of his death in 1842, Webster, a Yale scholar, had sold twenty-four million copies of his speller.

Lessons in arithmetic were learned from Colburn's *Intellectual Arithmetic,* or from *The Scholar's Arithmetic* by Jacob Willetts and others. Noah Webster did not rest with his "speller." He wrote *The History of the United States,* published in the 1830s, and offered it as a school textbook. There were others who wrote American history for school use, including Reverend C. A. Goodrich whose *History of the United States* enjoyed wide popularity. Another Goodrich—Samuel G. Goodrich— writing under the name of Peter Parley, contributed geography books which illustrated far off lands with exotic notions. One book showed a Chinese peddler selling unusual ingredients for pie-making—rats and puppies. Another Yale scholar, Jedidiah Morse, pioneered the study of modern geography.

Reading, writing, arithmetic, American history, world geography, lessons in civil behavior, and proper manners were the simple fare for simple common district schools. English, Latin, Greek, French, philosophy, elocution, and reading, writing, and arithmetic or some

GEOGRAPHY BOOK ILLUSTRATION

form of higher mathematics such as algebra or geometry were more advanced fare for more advanced schools—high schools and academies.

All of these subjects were taught in school terms that varied from a few weeks to nearly the entire length of the calendar year. However, most country district schools operated terms that included, roughly, December, January, and February for older children; and some two-and-a-half months during the summer for very small children. Sometimes these summer terms were run for young girls who either could not or would not attend the fall-winter term. The terms tended to be more frequent and longer in a city than in a rural area since the timing of a rural school term was geared to all of the chores and work that had to be done—the turning over of fields and planting in the spring; the early fall harvest; the preparations that had to be made at home to survive the long, cold winter, and more.

Generally, schools in the country districts could be characterized as having a single, crowded room, a mixture of ages and sexes often studying from different books side by side, a loose lesson plan overseen by a teenage teacher, and an unenforceable, ill kept, irregular attendance.

City schools tended to be larger and slightly more disciplined, but suffered from the same truancy and administrative problems, and a largely interested but unreliable public.

CLASSROOM AFTER THE CIVIL WAR

IV. THE WAR AND POST WAR YEARS: 1860–1900

In November, 1860, Abraham Lincoln was elected the sixteenth president of the United States. On March 4, 1861, he took the oath of office. A month later, on April 14th, Major Robert Anderson surrendered Fort Sumter, the Federal bastion in the harbor of Charleston, South Carolina, to Southern forces commanded by General Pierrre Beauregard. The Civil War had begun. Exactly four years from that date, April 14, 1865, Abraham Lincoln would be shot while sitting in his box at Ford's Theater in Washington, D.C.

During those four agonizing years, 1861–1865, little attention was devoted to the further development and improvement of American schools. America was in torment, split into two warring halves. Americans North and South were stunned by the ferocity of the fighting. As the conflict dragged on toward its inevitable conclusion, the entire country became spent and dazed by the tragedy of the struggle.

At Cold Harbor, Virginia, June 3, 1864, the Union Army under General Ulysses S. Grant assaulted the troops commanded by Robert E. Lee and suffered between six and seven thousand casualties in thirty minutes. Most of these were young men and teenage boys who not too many years before were using their trusty jackknives to carve their initials in some schoolhouse bench in search of boyish immortality. In 1864, such quick, overwhelming brutality was beyond belief.

Yet, despite the gloomy uncertainty of the deepening war, the Congress in Washington managed to enact a promising piece of legislation that would lay the foundation for publicly supported higher education throughout the United States. In 1862, it passed the Morrill,* or Land-Grant Act. This law gave to each state federally owned land to be used for the creation of state-run institutions devoted to college-level programs in agriculture, mechanics, and engineering.

While this was a seemingly innovative twist away from the traditional arts and humanities thrust of private higher education, a precedent had already been set as early as 1824 by the chartering of Rensselaer Polytechnic Institute, a private college of engineering in Troy, New York, the first institution in America to award a degree in engineering; by the founding of Brooklyn Polytechnic Institute in 1854, another private institution offering studies in engineering; by the founding of Michigan State College, East Lansing, in 1855, the first public institution to offer collegiate credit and degrees for studies in agriculture; and finally, the establishment of M.I.T.—Massachusetts Institute of Technology—in 1861, a private institution.

---

* Sponsored by Representative Justin S. Morrill of Vermont.

54

The passage of the Morrill Act in 1862, establishing the land-grant concept of higher education in which college programs would deal with the practical sciences, reflected a once growing but now urgent need. And that need was the ability of a vast country to respond to the challenge of the quickening changes being wrought by the Industrial Revolution and the trauma of modern warfare.

Many of those colleges created by the Morrill Act or, having been previously chartered, were aided by the donation of federal land under terms specified in the Act, and would eventually develop into quality institutions of higher learning. Among these were the Universities of California, Connecticut, Florida, Maine, Minnesota, Missouri, and Texas.

Following the Civil War, the pattern of the nation's varied local and state educational interests, already somewhat established, began to take on more definition. This definition clearly indicated a so-called "ladder system" that became fundamental to the American educational process. Essentially, the ladder system provided for a step by step advancement from compulsory elementary school to noncompulsory high school to noncompulsory college. Eventually, compulsory and noncompulsory education would be determined by age rather than by school, with the age of sixteen, for example, being an age beyond which a person could not be compelled to attend school.

The pattern of education consisted of two parallel tracks. One track belonged to the traditional costly private education, from Latin Grammar or lower schools to academies or college preparatory ("prep") schools to independent, self-supporting colleges and universities; from Boston Latin Grammar, for example, to Phillips Academy, to Harvard College. During the nineteenth century some five hundred or more independent, self-supporting colleges were established. One of these was Howard University in Washington, D.C.

Howard opened its doors in 1867 to provide higher education for black Americans, four years after the Emancipation Proclamation. In 1881, twenty-five-year-old Booker Taliaferro Washington, a self-educated former slave, founded a similar school for blacks in Alabama, Tuskegee Institute. The organizers of both institutions, Howard and Tuskegee, foresaw the struggle ahead of black Americans to achieve first class citizenship in a white country whose perception of them had been as non-citizens for more than two centuries. Black leaders quickly linked the political, economic, and social improvement of black Americans—like Americans of every other race, creed and persuasion—to education. But blacks were shut out of education, chiefly in the South where they were not permitted to enroll in existing schools restricted to "whites only." Black Americans were forced to confine their educational reach in the South to schools labelled "blacks only." And

BOOKER T. WASHINGTON

usually, these segregated schools did not possess a quality equal to the "white only" institutions. Segregation, in all its forms, would not be dissolved during the nineteenth century, and segregated education would be a major issue in American life well into the twentieth century.

The track parallel to private education belonged to publicly supported education. It was a less costly education, and hopefully, soon-to-be altogether free everywhere. Like private education, the ladder system here, too, provided for a step by step advancement from common or elementary school to high school, to land-grant college.

Although a number of America's larger cities had been mandated by their state lawmakers to provide free public elementary education since the 1830s, it was not until the 1850s and 1860s that cities like Albany, Baltimore, Chicago, New Orleans, and New York actually instituted workable free public schools supported by the collection of taxes from the general public.

While the rate bill system continued to fund public education in rural communities during the 1860s, more and more cities began collecting taxes to provide free education for their children following the end of the Civil War. And this they did despite the constant uproar of court battles testing the right of government— city, state, or federal—to tax an entire community for the education of part of the community.

A CITY PUBLIC SCHOOL ABOUT 1900

By 1870, the rate bill method of paying for one's education had seen better days and was all but finished. And in 1874, the United States Supreme Court handed down a landmark decision ruling that taxes could indeed be collected to support free public education at every level—elementary, high school, and college.

During the final years of the nineteenth century, the vast surge of European immigration, the growth of the cities, and the expansion of American industrial-technical know-how made education an imperative and fundamental right, central to the productivity and well-being of the country as a whole and each of its citizens. By 1900, the American public, compelled to participate in some form of free public elementary education, was better able to meet the challenge of change and the country's obvious and inevitable growth. But the ability to maintain that position into an unforeseeable and distant future was tied to the continuity and momentum of education and educational excellence beyond the usually minimal eight grades.

By the end of the century, there was a clear and indisputable link between America's security, her guarantee of domestic freedom, creativity, and productivity, and an educated public.

Index

American Speller, The, 49
Anderson, Major Robert, 53
Antioch College, 37

Barnard, Henry, 37, 38–43, 48
Bonaparte, Napoleon, 15
Boston Latin Grammar School, 7, 56
Brooklyn Polytechnic Institute, 54
Brown University, 13

Carter, James G., 30–31
charity schools, 12, 19
Civil War, 29, 44, 53–54, 55
Cleveland, Chauncey, 42
Clay, Henry, 27
Colburn, Warren, 49
College of Philadelphia, 12
College of William and Mary, The, 13, 16
Columbia University, 13
compulsory education, 8, 34, 37, 55

Dame Schools, 8
Dartmouth College, 13

Eclectic Reader, 29
Elementary Spelling Book, The, 49
Ellsworth, William W., 42
English School, The, 24–25

Franklin, Benjamin, 12
fraternities, 16

Goodrich, Rev. C. A., 49
Goodrich, Samuel G., 49
Grant, Ulysses S., 53

Harvard College, 7; University, 13, 56
History of the United States, 49
History of the United States, The, 49
horn book, 8
Howard University, 56

Industrial Revolution, 17–18, 24, 55
Intellectual Arithmetic, 49

Jackson, Andrew, 24, 25, 27

Land-Grant Act, see Morrill Act
Latin grammar schools, 7, 9, 12, 56
Lee, Robert E., 53
Lincoln, Abraham, 53
Lyon, Mary, 31

Mann, Horace, 32–37, 38, 48
Massachusetts Institute of Technology, 54
McGuffey, William Holmes, 28–29
"McGuffey's Reader," 29–30, 49
Michigan State College, 54
Morrill Act, 54, 55
Morrill, Justin S., 54
Morse, Jedidiah, 50
Mount Holyoke (Seminary) College, 30–32

New England Primer, 10
"normal schools," 31, 44

Oberlin College, 31

Parley, Peter, 49
Phi Beta Kappa, 16

Phillips Academy, 56
Princeton University, 13
public education (free), 9, 20–21, 23, 31, 34–36, 41–42, 44–45, 58, 60

religion, 7, 8, 10, 11, 12, 13, 35–36
Rensselaer Polytechnic Institute, 54
Rutgers University, 13

St. John's College, 43
Scholar's Arithmetic, The, 49
Schurz, Margaretha, 43
slavery, 20, 22, 23, 45
Sergeant, John, 27

Tuskegee Institute, 56

Union College, 15
unions, 21, 22–23
University of California, 55; Connecticut, 55; Florida, 55; Maine, 55; Minnesota, 55; Missouri, 55; Pennsylvania, 13; Texas, 55; Wisconsin, 42

Van Buren, Martin, 27
Virginia Assembly, 9

Washington, Booker T., 56, 57
Washington, George, 15
Webster, Noah, 49
Willetts, Jacob, 49

Yale University, 13

J
370
FISHER
  THE SCHOOLS

SAN LEANDRO COMMUNITY LIBRARY CENTER
SAN LEANDRO, CALIF.